Common Core Lessons & Activities:
Magnetism

By Carole Marsh

Published by Gallopade International, Inc.

Printed in the U.S.A. (Peachtree City, Georgia)

TABLE OF CONTENTS

G: Includes Graphic Organizer

GO: Graphic Organizer is also available 8½" x 11" online
download at www.gallopade.com/client/go
(numbers above correspond to the graphic organizer numbers online)

What Are Magnets?

Read the text and answer the questions.

You might have seen a magnet sticking to a refrigerator or on a desk. A magnet is an object that has the ability to attract or repel magnetic objects. When a magnet gets close to another magnetic object, the force of magnetism either pulls the object closer or pushes the object away. This pulling motion is called magnetic attraction, and the pushing motion is called magnetic repulsion.

Some magnets are natural and can be found in the Earth, but most magnets are artificial magnets made by people. Some magnets are permanent and will remain magnetic for a long time, and some magnets are temporary and can only be used for a short time. The type of magnet depends on the material the magnet is made from and the way the magnet is made.

Magnets are used in many ways you might not have realized. Car motors, refrigerator doors, ceiling fans, and computers are just a few of the places you might find them in your home. Magnets are also used in industry for tasks like generating electricity and separating metal scraps in junkyards. Electromagnets are special magnets created by the combination of electricity and magnetism. They play a central role in the work of electric motors. Did you know that the Earth itself is a giant magnet? We live inside the Earth's magnetic field, which stretches far out into space.

1. Match the following questions to whether they are best answered by paragraph 1, 2, or 3 of the text. Then answer each question.
   A. _______ How are magnets used by people?
   B. _______ What is a magnet?
   C. _______ What is the force that a magnet produces?
   D. _______ What are the different types of magnets?
   E. _______ What is magnetism?
   F. _______ What are electromagnets and how are they used?
   G. _______ How do magnets affect other magnetic objects?

2. Write at least three additional questions that you would like to know about magnetism. Share your questions with your class. Add additional questions based on the other questions you hear.

Reading for History

Read the text and answer the questions.

Thousands of years ago, ancient people noticed something unusual about a certain type of rock. In the 6th century B.C.E. a Greek scholar recorded his observations of how a certain rock was attracted to pieces of iron. Later, in the 4th century B.C.E., Chinese people observed the same thing from the same type of rock. They saw that some materials, like metals, were attracted to the rock but other materials, like grass or wood, were not.

In the 1st century C.E., the Chinese recorded new observations about this rock. They determined that the rock was a naturally magnetized piece of magnetite (a mineral that is naturally magnetic), and they called it a lodestone. They also discovered that if they floated a piece of lodestone in water or dangled it from a string, the lodestone always pointed north and south.

As a result of these important discoveries, the compass was invented. A compass includes a magnetized needle that always points north. By using a compass to determine which direction is north, other directions can also be determined.

Before the invention of the compass, sailors navigated by using star locations in the night sky. The compass made navigation more accurate, greatly improving exploration.

1. Write a title to accurately describe the main idea of this text.
2. What is the relationship between magnetite and lodestone?
3. A. How do historians know about the history of the lodestone?
   B. Make a simple table to record the century and observation of each discovery about the lodestone.
4. A. How did the Chinese discover that lodestones always point north and south?
   B. How is this knowledge useful for navigation?
5. The Age of Exploration was a time between the mid-1400s and mid-1600s C.E. when European explorers searched for new trade routes to Asia and discovered the Americas. What role do you think magnets played for sailors and explorers during this time? Why?

MAIN IDEA

Characteristics of Magnets

Read the text and answer the questions.

Magnets can attract (pull) certain objects without actually touching them. Magnets can also repel (push) certain objects without touching them. This push and pull is called magnetism. All magnets have an area around them, called a magnetic field, which is where the magnet has a pushing or pulling effect.

Every magnet has two ends, called poles. The poles are called north and south, or positive (+) and negative (–). If two magnets are placed so like poles (both north or both south) are near each other, they will repel each other. If they are placed so different poles are near (one north, one south), they will attract each other.

Magnets only attract objects that contain certain types of metals, such as iron, nickel, and cobalt. These objects are called magnetic because of their reaction to magnets. Most magnets are made of iron, or materials that contain iron, such as steel.

Some magnets are permanent, while other magnets are temporary. Electromagnets are temporary but remain magnetized as long as electricity flows.

1. Identify characteristics of magnets to complete the graphic organizer.

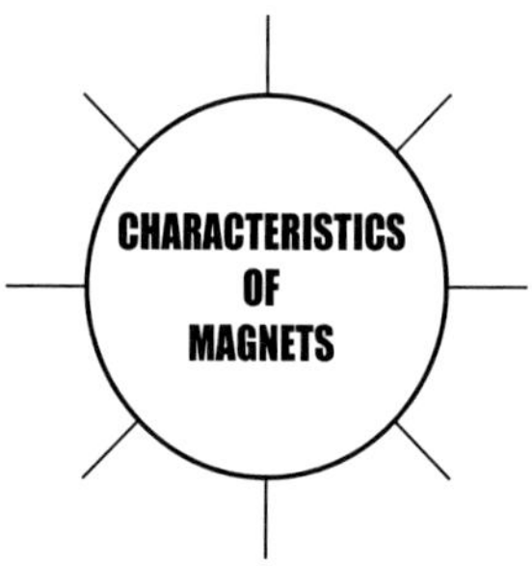

2. Design an experiment to test this hypothesis: "If a magnet is broken in half, each piece will also be a magnet." List materials you need; write clear steps of what you will do and what you will observe; and explain how you will determine if the hypothesis is correct.

The Power of Magnets

Read the texts and table and answer the questions.

Daryl conducted an experiment to investigate magnetic strength. He used four different magnets of different sizes and different metals. He tested for magnetic strength by measuring how many paper clips each magnet picked up—the more paper clips, the stronger the magnet.

Daryl summarized the results of his experiment in the table below.

Words to Know

alloy: a metal made by mixing two or more metals or a metal and another material

ferrous**: containing iron.

**Ferrous metals are the most common metals used to make magnets. However, some nonferrous metals including nickel and cobalt are also used to make magnets

Characteristics	Magnet A	Magnet B	Magnet C	Magnet D
Size	Small	Medium	Medium	Large
Made from	100% Iron	100% Nickel	50% Nickel 50% Cobalt	100% Iron
Number of paper clips picked up	10	14	17	24

1. Steel is a metal made of approximately 98% iron and 2% carbon.
   A. Is steel an alloy? Why or why not?
   B. Is steel ferrous? Why or why not?

2. Classify each of the magnets in the table as **ferrous** or **nonferrous**.
   A. ______________ C. ______________
   B. ______________ D. ______________

3. Were any of the magnets alloys? If so, which one(s)?

4. A. What is the purpose of the paper clips in the experiment?
   B. Which row of the table represents the strength of each magnet?
   C. Which magnet is strongest? How do you know?

5. According to Daryl's experiment, how does a magnet's size affect its strength?

6. According to Daryl's experiment, which is stronger—a pure nickel magnet or a magnetic alloy made of nickel and cobalt? Explain.

Attract & Repel

Read the texts and answer the questions.

Attract *verb*	**Repel** *verb*
1) To draw attention to oneself	1) To drive back or force away
2) To pull an object closer through use of a physical force	2) To be distasteful or repulsive to others
3) To be pleasing or alluring to others	3) To refuse or reject
4) To exert a pleasing influence	4) To push an object away through use of a physical force

Rules of Attraction and Repulsion

1) Two poles of opposite types will always attract one another.
2) Two poles of the same type will always repel each other.

1. A. Which definition of attract best explains the meaning of attract as it is used in the Rules of Attraction and Repulsion?
   B. Which definition of repel best explains the meaning of repel as it is used in the Rules of Attraction and Repulsion?

2. For each pair of words, determine whether their relationship is best described as antonyms or synonyms.
   A. attract, repel
   B. attract, pull
   C. repel, push
   D. pleasing, distasteful
   E. refuse, reject
   F. attraction, repulsion

3. Use the text to predict whether the magnets will attract or repel, and choose which Rule of Attraction and Repulsion supports your choice.

N | S S | N	N | S N | S
A. ____________________	B. ____________________

4. Match the use of each bold word below to the appropriate definition.
   A. ______“I was **attracted** to the idea of studying art in school.”
   B. ______“Hopefully the bug spray will **repel** the insects.”
   C. ______”These rain boots were made to **repel** water.”
   D. ______”The roller coaster **attracted** many people to the carnival.”
   E. ______”She was **repelled** by the smell of sour milk.”

COMPARE & CONTRAST

Permanent & Temporary Magnets

Read the text and answer the questions.

Magnets can be classified as either permanent or temporary.

Permanent magnets keep their magnetic properties once they have been magnetized. Permanent magnets often stay magnetized for a long time. However, permanent magnets can lose their magnetic properties. Heating a magnet to a high temperature, hammering a magnet, and rubbing a magnet with another magnet are some of the ways that permanent magnets can lose their magnetism.

Temporary magnets act like permanent magnets when they are within a strong magnetic field. However, they loose their magnetism when the field disappears. Any object that is attracted to a magnet becomes a temporary magnet while it is being attracted. When it is pulled away, it is no longer a magnet.

Electromagnets are also temporary magnets. An electromagnet (a magnet created using the force of electricity) remains magnetic as long as the current of electricity is flowing. When the power is turned off, the electromagnet is no longer a magnet.

1. Determine whether each magnet is a temporary or permanent magnet, and support your answer with information from the text.
   A. Magnetized iron ore found naturally in the ground; lodestone
   B. A magnetic picture frame
   C. A magnet created by an electric current running though a wire
2. A. What two forces cause objects to become temporary magnets?
   B. What happens to a temporary magnet when either of the forces is removed?
3. Read each statement and indicate whether it is true (T) or false (F). Then provide detailed information to explain why it is true or false.
   A. Electromagnets are permanent magnets.
   B. Permanent magnets always last forever.
   C. A paperclip is a magnet while it is attracted to a magnet.
   D. Electromagnets store up enough magnetism to last for a few hours in the case of a power outage.

How Does It Work?

Read the texts and answer the questions.

Why are some objects magnetized while others are not? Weber's Theory and Domain Theory are two popular theories that have been developed to explain why. Weber's Theory is based on the molecular alignment of material in a magnet. Domain Theory is a more modern explanation that is based on the motion of the electrons in the magnetic material.

Weber's Theory says that all magnetic substances contain tiny molecules called dipoles, and each dipole has a positive end and a negative end (like the poles of the magnet). Non-magnetized metals have messy dipoles that are arranged in a random order. Magnetized metals have their dipoles lined up where the positive ends all face the same direction, and the negative ends all face the opposite direction. The alignment of the dipoles gives an object its magnetic properties.

The Domain Theory says that magnetism is caused by the motion of electrons. Electrons are the part of an atom that circles around the nucleus. In non-magnetized metals, the electrons circle around the nucleus in different directions, half of the electrons moving one direction, and half moving the other direction. However, in the atoms of magnetized metals, more of the electrons revolve around the nucleus in one direction than in the other direction. It is this alignment of more than half of the electrons that gives an object its magnetic properties.

PART A: Answer these questions based on the first text.

1. What is the purpose of the two theories described in the text?
2. A. Use the text to define dipoles.
   B. What do dipoles have in common with magnets?
3. A. Which theory is primarily based on alignment of dipoles?
   B. Which theory is primarily based on motion of electrons?
4. Summarize each of the theories in your own words.

5. Match each of the following descriptions to the correct diagram.
   A. non-magnetized dipoles
   B. magnetized dipoles
   C. non-magnetized atom
   D. magnetized atom

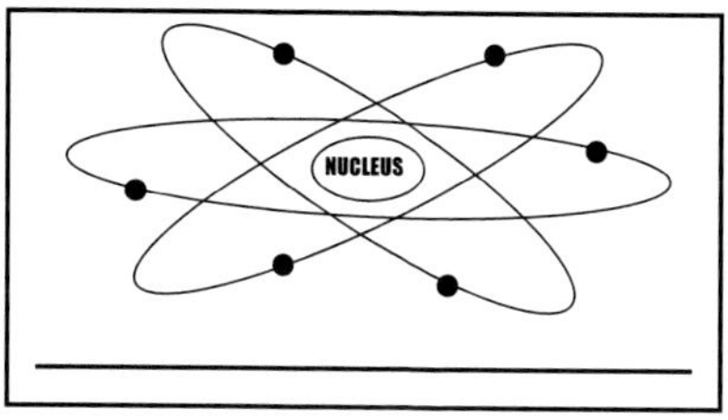

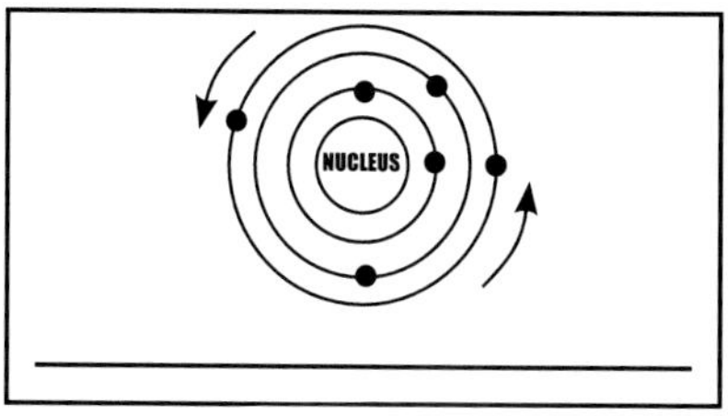

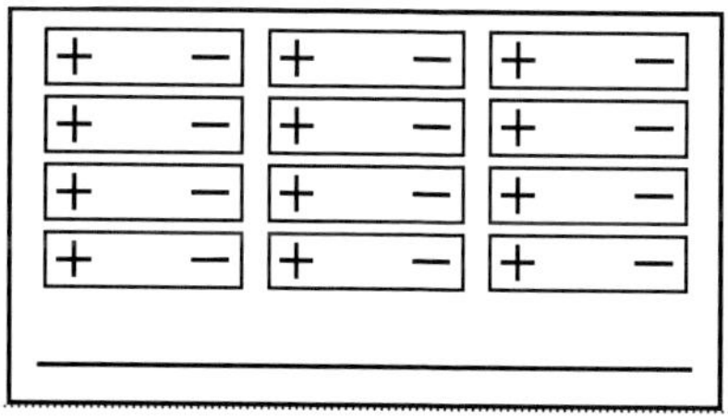

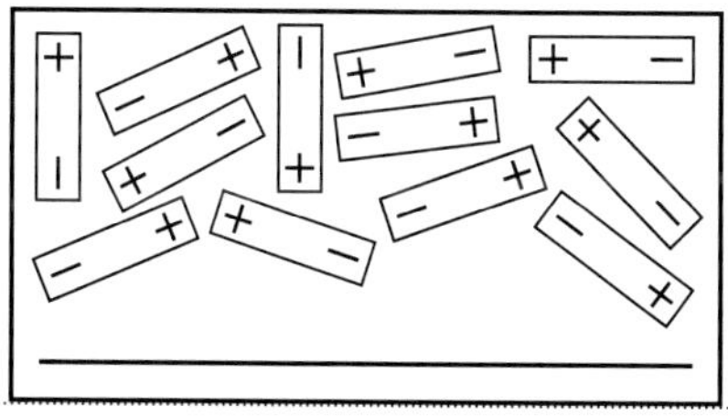

PART B: Use what you have learned to analyze the text and answer these questions.

Some magnets are naturally occurring in the Earth, but most magnets are created. To turn a non-magnetized steel bar into a magnet, rub a magnet against the steel bar several times, each time rubbing in the same direction. The non-magnetized steel bar will become magnetized!

6. A. Use Weber's Theory to describe what happens when you turn a steel bar into a magnet.
   B. Draw a diagram to illustrate the change that occurs.
7. A. Use the Domain Theory to describe what is happening.
   B. Draw a diagram to illustrate the change that occurs.
8. If the steel bar that was magnetized eventually loses its magnetism, describe what must have occurred according to:
   A. Weber's Theory
   B. Domain Theory
9. Do you think rubbing a magnet across a steel bar in random directions would cause the steel bar to become magnetized? Why or why not?
10. Do you think rubbing a magnet across a metal paperclip would cause the paperclip to become magnetized? Why or why not?

Magnetic Fields

Read the text and answer the questions.

A magnetic field is the space around a magnet in which the magnet's force will work. A magnet's power to push and pull only reaches as far as its magnetic field. A magnetic field is invisible, but the effects of a magnetic field can be seen and measured.

A magnetic field reaches outward from a magnet, along paths that scientists call lines of force. Lines of force travel around a magnet from the magnet's north pole to the magnet's south pole. This direction of magnetic force is what causes the north pole of one magnet to be attracted to the south pole of another magnet, and it is what causes two like poles to repel each other.

Some magnets are strong and some magnets are weak. The magnetic field of a strong magnet can pull or push objects from a much greater distance than the magnetic field of a weak magnet. Large magnets are typically stronger than small magnets and have lines of force that reach greater distances.

1. Use the text to explain the concept of a magnetic field.
2. How do scientists know that a magnetic field exists?
3. Use the text to label each of the following items on the diagram:
   _____ magnet's north pole
   _____ magnet's south pole
   _____ magnet's center
   _____ magnet's lines of force

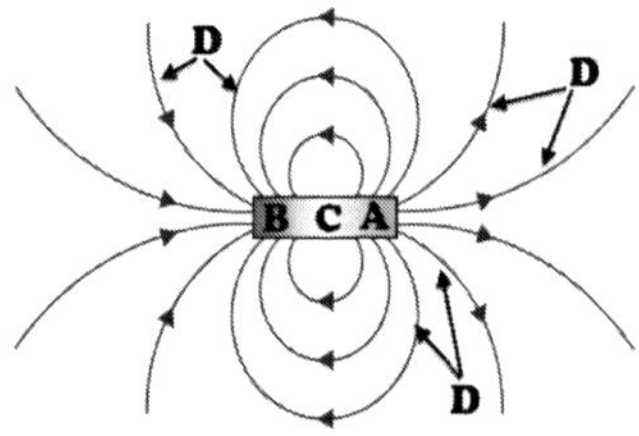

4. A. How does a magnet's size affect its lines of force?
   B. How does a magnet's power affect its lines of force?
5. Describe what is happening in each diagram below, and explain why.

A.

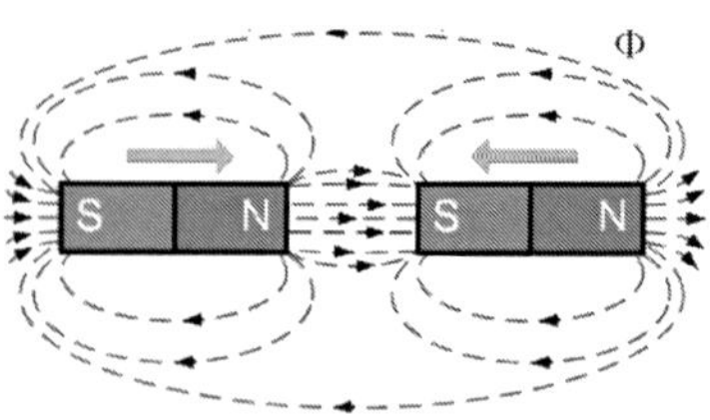

B.

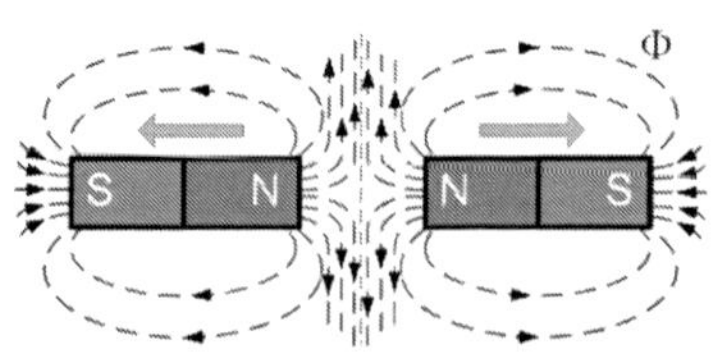

EXPERIMENT ANALYSIS

Magnetic Pull

Read the text, look at the chart, and answer the questions.

Jeremy designed an experiment using a bar magnet and several paper clips. He placed paper clips around the magnet, and as he did, he recorded how strongly the magnet pulled on each one. He drew a diagram to show the location of each paper clip, and he recorded his observations in an observation chart.

PAPER CLIP	OBSERVATION
A	immediate strong pull
B	no pull at all
C	weak pull
D	very weak pull
E	moderate pull
F	very weak, almost no pull
G	Immediate strong pull

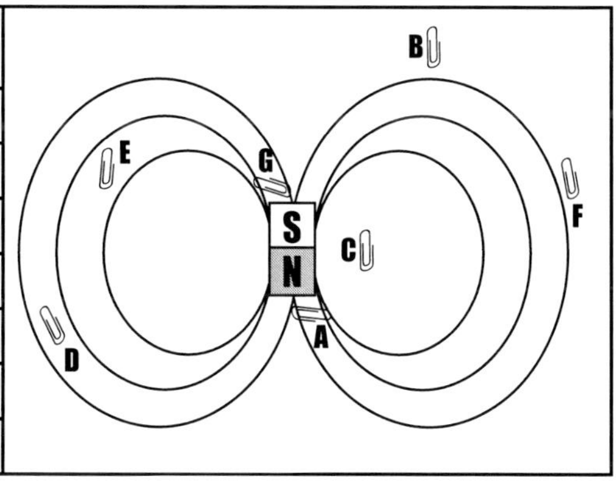

1. What was the purpose of Jeremy's experiment?
2. What is the purpose of Jeremy's diagram?
3. A. What was the independent variable in the experiment?
   B. What was the dependent variable in the experiment?
4. Read each conclusion statement and determine whether it **supports** (**S**) or **contradicts** (**C**) the evidence in the chart:
   A. _____ A magnetic field is strongest near a magnet's center.
   B. _____ A magnetic field is strongest near a magnet's poles.
   C. _____ A magnet does not affect objects beyond its magnetic field.
   D. _____ A magnet's north pole is stronger than its south pole.
   E. _____ Objects that are farther away from a magnet are affected less by the pull of the magnetic field than objects that are close.
   F. _____ Objects in a magnetic field are pulled equally regardless of their location.

Magnetism

Complete the graphic organizer by identifying sources, characteristics, and effects of magnetism.

Sources: **Characteristics**

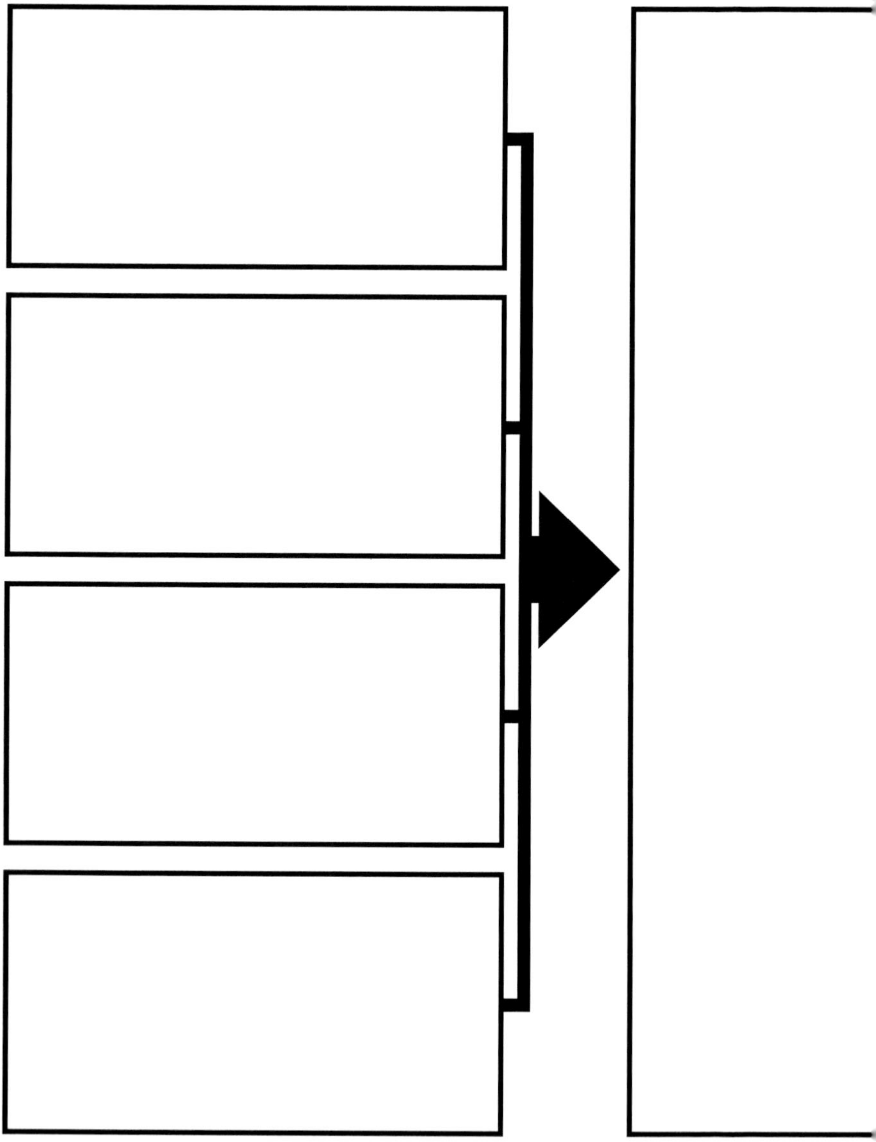

of Magnetism:

Effects:

History of Electromagnetism

Read the text and answer the questions.

Before the 1800s, most people thought that electricity and magnetism were two very different things. Scientists in the early 1800s made many important discoveries that led to the realization that electricity and magnetism are closely related.

In the early 1800s, a scientist in Denmark named Hans Christian Oersted discovered that a magnetic needle reacted to a nearby electric current. He determined that electric currents create their own magnetic field.

Around 1820, a French scientist named Andre Marie Ampere discovered that parallel electrical wires could attract and repel like magnets, depending on whether the currents flowed in the same or opposite direction. Ampere saw this as proof that electricity produced a form of magnetism with attracting and repelling poles.

And in 1831, British scientist Michael Faraday discovered that moving a magnet near a wire coil causes an electric current to flow through the wire. This discovery suggested that magnetism and electricity are connected parts of an interrelated natural process. Faraday recognized that magnets do not create electricity—they cause electricity to flow. His discovery led to the invention of the electric motor, which is used to power cars, appliances, and more.

1. A. What is the main idea of the text?
   B. Describe how the author develops the main idea.
2. Create a table to summarize the information about the scientists. Include a title to describe how the scientists relate to each other. Include who they were, where they were from, when they lived, and what they discovered about magnetism.
3. A. What conclusion did Oersted draw from his observation?
   B. What conclusion did Ampere draw from his observation?
   C. What conclusion did Faraday draw from his observation?
4. Why is it significant that Faraday recognized magnets do not create electricity, when there was no previous assumption that they did?
5. Cite evidence from each scientist's observations to support the statement: "Magnetism and electricity are two sides of the same coin."

CONCEPTS & PROCESSES

Characteristics of Electromagnets

Read the text and answer the questions.

Electromagnets are a special type of magnet, but they have the key characteristics of magnetism, just like a bar magnet. An electromagnet has a north pole and a south pole. It can attract and repel objects. And, it creates a magnetic field with lines of force just like a bar magnet. However, electromagnets are made differently and used differently than bar magnets.

A simple electromagnet is created by running an electric current through a wire. The electric current has its own electromagnetic field and creates a weak magnetism. If the wire is then wrapped like a coil, it becomes what is called a solenoid. The magnetic field within the solenoid coil is even stronger than the original magnetic field. If the coils are wrapped around a magnetic material like iron, nickel, or cobalt, the strength of the electromagnet increases even more. A larger magnetic core and more solenoid coils cause the magnet to become even stronger.

So what makes electromagnets so important? It is their ability to be easily turned on and off. Unlike a bar magnet, which is a permanent magnet, electromagnets are temporary magnets that only hold their charge as long as electricity flows through them. As a result, they have unique uses. They are commonly used in items such as computers, cars, telephones, appliances, and more.

1. A. How are bar magnets and electromagnets similar?
   B. How are bar magnets and electromagnets different?
2. A. What creates an electromagnetic field?
   B. List two ways that an electromagnetic field can be made stronger.
3. Look at the diagram of the simple electromagnet created in 1824 by British scientist William Sturgeon.
   A. What is represented by arrows A?
   B. What is represented by arrows B?
   C. What is represented by arrow C?

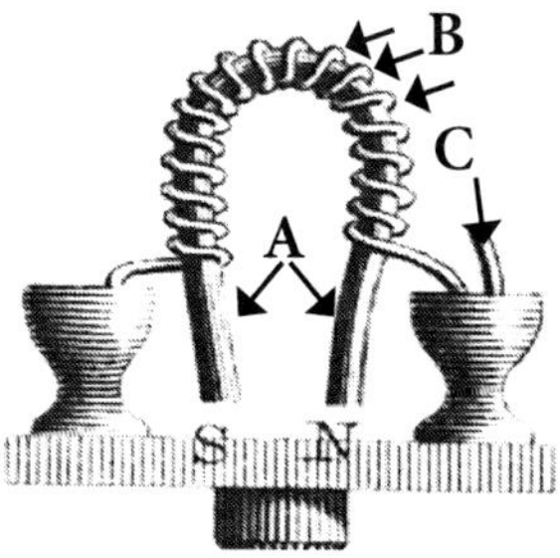

4. Explain how you could make this electromagnet stronger.

Magnetic Mechanism

Look at the diagram and answer the questions.

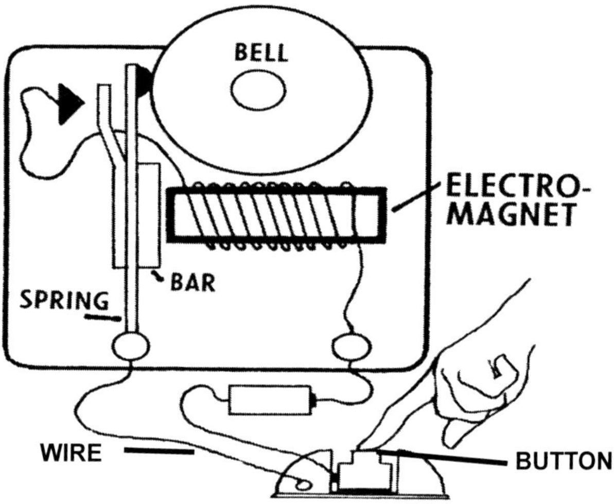

1. What is the purpose of each of the following parts of the machine?
   A. The wire
   B. The electromagnet
   C. The spring
   D. The bell
2. List at least 5 devices in which a machine like this might be used.
3. Number the events below in the proper sequence:

_____ The electric current runs through the solenoid coils.

_____ The metal bar is held away from the bell by a spring.

_____ The button is pressed, allowing electricity to flow through the wire.

_____ When the button is released, the electric current turns off.

_____ The electromagnet becomes magnetized.

_____ The electromagnetic demagnetizes and the bar returns to its resting position.

_____ The metal bar is pulled towards the electromagnet, causing the bar to strike the bell.

Uses of Magnets

Describe how each device uses magnetism. Use an online resource to identify any unfamiliar devices.

MAGNETIC-LEVITATION TRAIN ON TRACKS

INDUSTRIAL MAGNET MOVING SCRAP METAL

COMPASS

MAGNETIC KNIFE RACK

1. A. Which of the four devices make use of permanent magnets?
   B. Which of the four devices make use of electromagnets?
   C. Which devices use the attracting force of magnetism?
   D. Which device uses the repelling force of magnetism? (Hint: It uses it to reduce friction.)
2. Explain how magnets might be used to solve each problem.
   A. A cabinet door will not stay shut.
   B. Metal nails on the ground near a construction site cause flat tires.
   C. In a food processing factory, small pieces of metal sometimes fall into the food.
   D. An airport is enlarging and needs a way to quickly get passengers from check-in to the gate where they board their plane.

COMPARISON OF SOURCES

Earth's Magnetic Field

Read the texts and answer the questions.

The Earth is surrounded by its own magnetic field. In fact, the Earth acts like one giant magnet! Like all magnets, the Earth has a north pole and a south pole. Also like all magnets, the Earth's magnetic field has invisible lines of force that travel from the north pole around the body of the magnet to the south pole.

What causes the Earth's magnetism? Deep inside the Earth is the Earth's core. The Earth's core is made of two parts—inner core and outer core. The inner core is solid iron about 760 miles thick. The outer core is a layer of hot liquid iron, nickel, and other metals about 1,408 miles thick that swirls around inside the Earth. The molten metal in the outer core moves in currents, cooling and heating, rising and falling. As the molten metal moves, it causes electric currents. Charged metals that move through these electric currents create electric currents of their own, and the cycle continues. This self-sustaining loop is known as the geodynamo. The Earth's spin causes the movement in the outer core to result in the magnetic fields being aligned in the same direction, all adding up to one great big magnet! This field wraps around the Earth like a bubble and is called the magnetosphere.

1. What characteristics of a magnet does the Earth have?
2. A. Name and describe the two parts of the Earth's core.
   B. What is the most significant difference between the two parts?
3. A. Use the text to define self-sustaining.
   B. What causes the geodynamo to be self-sustaining?
4. A. Use the text to define magnetosphere.
   B. What simile is used to describe the Earth's magnetosphere?
5. Combine information from the text with what you already know about magnets and magnetic fields to create a diagram of the Earth's magnetic poles and magnetic field, including lines of force.
6. What factor causes the electric currents generated in the inner core of the Earth to result in the Earth's magnetic field?

This illustration is a drawing by French Philosopher Rene Descartes from 1644. It shows the magnetic field (D) of the Earth attracting several round loadstones (I, K, L, M, N). Descartes believed that magnetism was caused by tiny thread-like particles too small to see. He thought that these threadlike particles came out of a magnet from the north end and traveled around the magnet, and passed through holes in the lodestones, pulling them or pushing them.

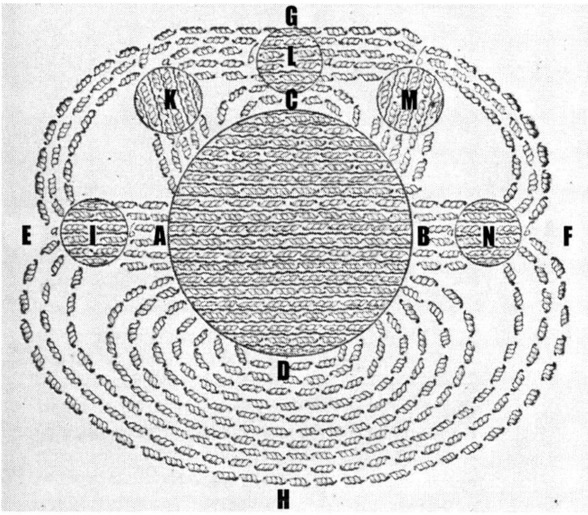

7. A. What was Descartes' purpose for creating this illustration?
   B. Who might have been the intended audience?

8. A. What did Descartes believe caused the Earth's magnetism?
   B. Which part of the diagram illustrates the Earth's magnetic field?

9. A. Which part of the diagram illustrates the Earth's lines of force?
   B. How does Rene Descartes' illustration of the Earth's lines of force compare with your own? Describe any similarities or differences.

10. Which parts of Rene Descartes' theory of Earth's magnetism are close to being scientifically correct?

11. Which parts of Rene Descartes' theory of Earth's magnetism are far from the scientific truth?

Writing Prompt:

Rene Descartes was scientist who emphasized using reason to understand causes in nature. Why is Descartes' theory of magnetism important to science, even if parts of it are wrong? Write a short paragraph using logical reasoning to support your answer. As a class, discuss the importance of using reason to build scientific knowledge.

The Magnetosphere

Read the texts and answer the questions.

Water, oxygen, and a mild temperature are all things that make life on Earth possible. But, magnetism plays an essential role too. The Earth's magnetic field, also called the magnetosphere, acts like a [1]shield against dangerous high-energy particles from the sun called [2]solar wind. The magnetosphere directs the solar wind safely around the Earth, but not without effect. Solar wind causes the Earth's magnetosphere to bend. On one side, the magnetosphere is [3]compressed into a small field. On the opposite side, the magnetosphere is [4]stretched out.

The Earth's magnetosphere helps us find our way! Humans often use a compass to navigate. A compass' north-pointing magnetic needle uses the Earth's magnetic field. Many scientists believe that some animals have a natural "internal compass" that also uses Earth's magnetic field for navigation. For example, migrating birds know which direction to fly in the winter, and sea turtles find their way back to where they lay eggs every year.

1. A. What is the common theme between the two texts?
   B. Write a descriptive title for each text.
2. Match each part of the diagram to the descriptive phrase numbered in the first text.

   A. ______

   B. ______

   C. ______

   D. ______

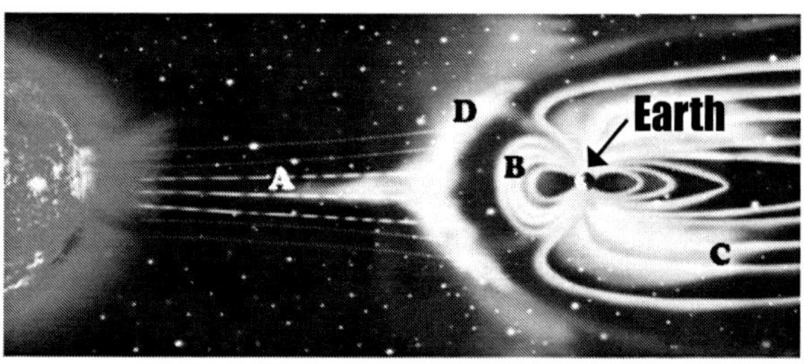

3. What does the phrase "internal compass" mean in the text.
4. Predict the effect on each item if the Earth lost its magnetism.
   A. compasses B. migrating birds C. life on earth.

EXPERIMENT ANALYSIS

Can You Pick It Up?

PART A: With a partner, collect all of the objects listed in the chart. Sort the objects into groups. You might group objects based on size, weight, shape, material, or some other criteria you choose.

PART B: As a class, discuss the different characteristics that were used to sort the objects, and how easy or difficult it was to determine which items went into which groups. List three methods that were used, and describe how precise or imprecise those classification methods were.

PART C: Predict which items will be attracted to a magnet (magnetic) and which items will not be (non-magnetic), and record this in the chart.

PART D: Slowly touch each item with a bar magnet. Record your observations in the chart, and then answer the questions that follow.

Item	Prediction	Observed Effect of Magnet
paper clip		
toothpick		
notebook paper		
dime		
penny		
plastic cup		
scissors		
pen		
pencil		
staples		

1. A. Which items are magnetic? What did they have in common?
   B. Which items are non-magnetic? What did they have in common?
   C. Did any items seem more magnetic than others? Describe.
2. Based on your observations, which characteristics were common in the items that were magnetic? (size, shape, weight, material, etc.)
3. Write a hypothesis for a new experiment based on your analysis.

Magnet Misconceptions

Rewrite each misconception to be accurate.

MISCONCEPTION: A magnet broken in half will result in two pieces – one with a north pole and the other with a south pole.
TRUE FACT:
MISCONCEPTION: Magnets create electricity.
TRUE FACT:
MISCONCEPTION: An electromagnet must have an iron core.
TRUE FACT:
MISCONCEPTION: Magnets do not occur naturally and must be created.
TRUE FACT:
MISCONCEPTION: All metals are attracted to magnets.
TRUE FACT:
MISCONCEPTION: The earth's magnetic and geographic poles are located in the same location.
TRUE FACT:
MISCONCEPTION: Only magnets produce magnetic fields.
TRUE FACT:

Magnetism Vocabulary

Just like magnetic poles, these words and phrases want to attract their opposites. Match each magnetism vocabulary word or phrase to the word or phrase that means the opposite. Then write a sentence to explain the meaning of the words or phrases that are paired together.

GEOGRAPHICAL NORTH POLE

RANDOM DIPOLES

NEGATIVE CHARGE

MAGNETIZED DIPOLES

METALS CONTAINING NO IRON

NATURAL MAGNET

PERMANENT MAGNET

FERROUS METALS

REPULSION

MAGNETIC NORTH POLE

MANMADE MAGNET

POSITIVE CHARGE

TEMPORARY MAGNET

ATTRACTION

Correlations to Common Core State Standards

For your convenience, correlations are listed page-by-page, and for the entire book!

This book is correlated to the Common Core State Standards for English Language Arts grades 3-8, and to Common Core State Standards for Literacy in History, Science, & Technological Subjects grades 6-8.

Correlations are highlighted in gray. (Highlighted numbers are shown in bold below.)

PAGE #	READING *Includes:* RI: Reading Informational Text RST: Reading Science & Technical Subjects	WRITING *Includes:* W: Writing WHST: Writing History/Social Studies, Science, & Technical Subjects	LANGUAGE *Includes:* L: Language LF: Language Foundational Skills	SPEAKING & LISTENING *Includes:* SL: Speaking & Listening
2	RI/RST . **1** **2** 3 **4** **5** 6 7 8 9 **10**	W/WHST . 1 **2** 3 4 5 6 7 **8** 9 **10**	L/LF . 1 2 3 **4** 5 **6**	SL . **1** 2 3 4 5 6
3	RI/RST . **1** **2** **3** **4** **5** 6 7 **8** 9 **10**	W/WHST . 1 **2** 3 **4** 5 6 7 **8** **9** **10**	L/LF . 1 2 3 **4** 5 **6**	SL . 1 2 3 4 5 6
4	RI/RST . **1** **2** **3** **4** 5 6 7 8 9 **10**	W/WHST . 1 **2** **3** **4** **5** 6 **7** 8 9 **10**	L/LF . 1 2 3 **4** **5** **6**	SL . 1 2 3 4 5 6
5	RI/RST . **1** **2** **3** **4** **5** **6** **7** **8** **9** **10**	W/WHST . 1 **2** 3 **4** 5 6 7 8 9 10	L/LF . 1 2 3 **4** 5 **6**	SL . 1 2 3 4 5 6
6	RI/RST . **1** **2** **3** **4** **5** 6 **7** 8 **9** **10**	W/WHST . 1 **2** 3 **4** 5 6 7 8 **9** **10**	L/LF . 1 2 **3** **4** **5** **6**	SL . 1 2 3 4 5 6
7	RI/RST . **1** 2 **3** **4** **5** 6 7 **8** 9 **10**	W/WHST . 1 **2** 3 **4** 5 6 7 8 9 **10**	L/LF . 1 2 3 **4** **5** **6**	SL . 1 2 3 4 5 6
8-9	RI/RST . **1** **2** **3** **4** **5** 6 **7** 8 9 **10**	W/WHST . **1** **2** 3 **4** 5 6 7 **8** **9** **10**	L/LF . 1 2 3 **4** **5** **6**	SL . 1 2 3 4 5 6
10	RI/RST . **1** **2** **3** 4 **5** 6 **7** **8** **9** **10**	W/WHST . 1 **2** 3 **4** 5 6 7 8 **9** **10**	L/LF . 1 2 3 **4** 5 **6**	SL . 1 2 3 4 5 6
11	RI/RST . **1** **2** **3** 4 **5** 6 **7** **8** **9** **10**	W/WHST . 1 **2** 3 **4** 5 6 7 8 9 **10**	L/LF . 1 2 3 4 5 6	SL . 1 2 3 4 5 6
12-13	RI/RST . 1 2 3 **4** **5** 6 7 8 **9** **10**	W/WHST . 1 **2** 3 **4** 5 6 7 8 9 **10**	L/LF . 1 2 3 **4** **5** **6**	SL . 1 2 3 4 5 6
14	RI/RST . **1** **2** **3** **4** **5** **6** 7 **8** 9 **10**	W/WHST . 1 **2** 3 **4** 5 6 7 **8** **9** **10**	L/LF . 1 2 3 **4** **5** **6**	SL . 1 2 3 4 5 6
15	RI/RST . **1** **2** **3** **4** **5** 6 **7** 8 **9** **10**	W/WHST . 1 **2** 3 **4** 5 6 7 8 **9** **10**	L/LF . 1 2 3 **4** 5 **6**	SL . 1 2 3 4 5 6
16	RI/RST . 1 **2** **3** 4 **5** 6 **7** 8 9 **10**	W/WHST . 1 **2** 3 4 5 6 7 **8** **9** **10**	L/LF . 1 2 3 4 5 6	SL . 1 2 3 4 5 6
17	RI/RST . 1 2 **3** **4** **5** 6 **7** 8 9 **10**	W/WHST . 1 **2** 3 **4** 5 6 7 8 9 10	L/LF . 1 2 3 **4** **5** **6**	SL . 1 2 3 4 5 f
18-19	RI/RST . **1** **2** **3** **4** **5** **6** **7** **8** **9** **10**	W/WHST . **1** **2** **3** **4** 5 **6** **7** **8** **9** **10**	L/LF . 1 2 3 **4** **5** **6**	SL . **1** **2** 3 4 5 6
20	RI/RST . 1 **2** **3** **4** 5 6 **7** **8** **9** **10**	W/WHST . 1 **2** 3 **4** 5 6 7 8 9 **10**	L/LF . 1 2 3 **4** **5** **6**	SL . 1 2 3 4 5 6
21	RI/RST . **1** **2** 3 4 **5** 6 7 8 9 **10**	W/WHST . 1 **2** 3 **4** **5** 6 **7** **8** **9** **10**	L/LF . 1 2 3 4 5 6	SL . **1** **2** 3 **4** 5 **6**
22	RI/RST . 1 **2** 3 4 5 6 7 8 9 **10**	W/WHST . 1 **2** 3 **4** 5 6 7 **8** 9 **10**	L/LF . 1 2 3 **4** 5 **6**	SL . **1** 2 3 4 5 6
23	RI/RST . 1 2 3 **4** 5 6 7 8 9 10	W/WHST . 1 **2** 3 4 5 6 7 8 9 10	L/LF . 1 2 3 **4** 5 **6**	SL . 1 2 3 4 5 6
COMPLETE BOOK	RI/RST . **1** **2** **3** **4** **5** **6** **7** **8** **9** **10**	W/WHST . **1** **2** **3** **4** **5** **6** **7** **8** **9** **10**	L/LF . 1 2 **3** **4** **5** **6**	SL . **1** **2** 3 **4** 5 **6**

For the complete Common Core standard identifier, combine your grade + "." + letter code above + "." + number code above.

In addition to the correlations indicated here, the activities may be adapted or expanded to align to additional standards and to meet the diverse needs of your unique students!